Two Sovereign Hearts

Poetry of an Unapologetic Life

Laqshyajit Rai

/ BookLeaf
Publishing

India | USA | UK

Made with ❤ on the BookLeaf Publishing Platform

www.bookleafpub.in

www.bookleafpub.com

Dedication

For the women who came before me, whose voices were
silenced, whose dreams were buried before they could
bloom.
For those still searching for the true meaning of love, and
for the dreamers who dare to dream big,
may these words remind you
that *your story matters*,
your voice matters,
you matter.

Preface

This book is not a collection of perfect poems.
It is a collection of lived truths.
These poems are pieces of my life,
the messy, honest, beautiful kind of love and resilience
that money can't buy
and time cannot erase.

Every page carries a fragment of my journey
the shy girl who once traveled miles to meet her
soulmate,
the daughter raised by a fierce single mother,
the woman who learned to see rain not just as romance
but as reality,
the lover who ate bhelpuri on a 130-rupee date
and later celebrated life at JW Marriott,
the wife who built a home out of love and trust, not
bricks,
and the dreamer who walked away from safety
to follow the voice of her own soul.

These poems are about love
not the kind sold in movies or social media,
but the kind that shows up at 3 a.m. with Maggi,
that saves for months to buy a first car,

that holds you when farewells make you cry,
that says "I believe in you" louder than the world's
doubts.

They are also about inheritance
the silence of women who came before me,
their tears, their unspoken dreams,
and the choice I made to refuse to pass that pain
forward.

This book is for anyone who has ever believed
that love is more than money,
that strength is born from struggle,
and that joy can be found
in the smallest, simplest things.

It is for those who know that life is not always grand
but when it is ours, it is enough.

Acknowledgements

To my husband, my best friend, my greatest cheerleader,
my steady hand, my safe place.
This book would not exist without your quiet strength,
your endless patience, and your unwavering belief in me,
even when I doubted myself. Thank you for teaching me
that love is not spoken, it is lived.

To Cooper, my furry boy, you reminded me of the
simplest truths: to love without conditions, to find joy in
the smallest things, and to live fully in every fleeting
moment. You have been one of my gentlest teachers.

To my mother, the fiercest woman I know. Who carried
storms on her shoulders
yet raised me to stand tall, to live life on my own terms,
and to never apologize for my truth.
Your resilience runs through my veins.

To my late father-in-law, a man ahead of his time. Who
saw the world differently,
who believed in fairness, who gave respect where many
only gave rules.
Your spirit continues to guide us toward a life lived with
dignity and openness.

And to my late grandfather, the first man who believed
in me before the world ever did.
Your faith in me planted seeds I still carry, and every
page of this book is a whisper of gratitude to you.

This book belongs to you all.
A reflection of love, loyalty, lessons, and the courage to
dream
for the ones who walked beside me,
for the one who waits at the door with wagging tail,
and for the ones watching from above.

1. Second Daughter, First Rebel

I was born a second daughter.
And in that moment,
my mother's joy was stolen.

She told me later
the women in our family
were not happy either.
And now
another one,
another girl,
another sigh in the community ledger.

Everyone consoled her:
It will be a boy next time.
Try again, they said,
as if daughters are failed attempts,
as if we arrive broken,
unworthy of celebration.

Because girls
we are still seen as responsibilities,
never as individuals.
And the silence of suppressed dreams,
the hush of tolerated abuse,
the smiles that never reached the eyes
they were passed down
like family heirlooms.

So trauma
it didn't start with me.
It started with all the women before me.
It trickled down,
generation after generation,
until it found my mother.
And then
it found me.
The second daughter.

But here is where it stops.
With me.
I will not bow under that weight.
I will not carry this inheritance of sorrow.
I will not be the quiet,
the shadow,
the tolerated abuse,
the smile that hides the wound.

I will be the break in the chain.
I will be the loud refusal.
I will be the one who says:

A daughter is not a curse.
A daughter is not a burden.
A daughter is not a failed attempt.

I am the second daughter.
And I am the first woman
in my line
to set us free.

2. Her Strength, My Fire

She wore strength like second skin,
not because life made it easy,
but because three little faces
looked up at her
with hunger, with hope,
with trust too fragile to break.

She never asked.
Never begged.
Her hands carried the weight of worlds
in silence,
while her feet kept moving
always on her toes,
always chasing tomorrow
before it could slip away.

Three children,
A single mother,
And a battlefield dressed as home.
She stood in the center

shield and sword in one,
love and discipline in the other.

Against odds that sneered,
against nights that stretched too long,
she stitched a life
out of grit and sacrifice,
teaching me not just to survive,
but to live
on my own terms.

She showed me that freedom
isn't given,
It's carved.
That dignity
isn't asked for,
it's claimed.
That no matter the storm,
We carry our own fire.

I am my mother's child
not just her blood,
but her rebellion,
her resilience,
her dream continued.
And when I stand tall,
I know

it is her strength
that steadied my spine.

3. 368 Kilometres to Destiny

A girl once traveled **three hundred sixty-eight kilometers**
not knowing she was moving toward her soulmate.
She was only listening
to something quiet,
yet certain,
inside her heart.

Who would have thought?
A daughter of the valleys of **Jammu**
finding home in the heartbeat of a **Haryanvi-Punjabi boy.**
A concoction never dreamt of
but aren't the best things in life
always unplanned?

Inside me lived a girl,
secretly shy, naïve, yet strangely bold,
a girl who had spent years
letting life happen to her.
And then one day
She decided to own her story.

And the Universe leaned close, smirked and whispered:
"You're ready."

And what it handed me...
was more than I could ever dream.
He was young.
But he carried his world like a man.
A provider.
A giver.
Raised in struggle,
yet rich,
rich in compassion.

And then he met me
a girl with a scarred past,
I came with barbed wire around my heart.
A past heavy enough to choke.
I was scarred,
sharp-edged,
hard to hold.

It wasn't easy.
Hell no.
I didn't make it easy either.
I pushed him away
again,
again,

And again.

Fear louder than love.
Habit heavier than hope.
And this belief
that girls like me don't deserve
soft love.

But he stayed.
Do you hear me?
He. Stayed.
Patient.
Steady.
Gentle.

And his consistency?
It was water against stone.
It cracked me open
not all at once,
but piece by piece.

Until one day
through the wreckage of all my walls
love walked in.
Soft. Certain.
And Unshakable.

4. A Place to Be

She called herself a hopeless romantic,
Dreaming of love, soft and tragic.
The pages of novels, filled with sweet lies,
Where hearts found solace under starry skies.

But her childhood, a storm she couldn't outrun,
Her parent's separation, the damage done.
She learned early to trust with care,
To guard her heart, to never share.

Her father's disappointment, her deepest scar,
Made her question how love could go so far.
She didn't expect much, just a space to breathe,
A home of her own, where she could believe.

Then came him, the one who had no time,
A responsible son, his life in climb.
At sixteen, he carried his family's weight,
A boy shaped by struggle, shaped by fate.

His childhood lost in the grind of the day,
Two jobs in hand, dreams locked away.
He never asked for much, never made a plea,
Selfless, always giving, never free.

They met, two souls from different walks,
Her heart guarded, his full of talks.
But in the quiet, when no words were needed,
She found in his silence, a love unimpeded.

For she wanted more than just a fairytale's end,
A love where they didn't have to pretend.
In his eyes, she saw a home she could trust,
A place to be herself, where hearts could adjust.

He never promised her forever,
But in his arms, she found her tether.
Not just a man, but someone who knew,
What it was to survive, and still break through.

She, the hopeless romantic, with scars to heal,
And he, the selfless boy, is learning to feel.
Together, they built something simple, yet true
A love, in the quiet, where dreams could renew.

5. Can I drop you home

Can I drop you home?
he messaged, casual-almost too casual.
She smiled,
"I'm already home."

A blink.
A beat.
Disappointment parked in silence.
"Tomorrow then?"
Nervous. Soft. Hopeful.
"Sure," she said.

The office air buzzed,
but not louder than their glances.
A corner smile here,
a quiet nod there
both trying not to be
too obvious,
and failing just enough.

Evening came.
She walked toward his car
He'd cleaned it.
The playlist? Curated.
His heart? Racing.

They drove.
Five minutes turned to fifteen.
"You just passed my home!"
she laughed, mock-shocked.
He smirked, eyes on the road,
"You didn't really think
I was just driving you home?"
She didn't answer.
But her smile said:
"I was hoping not."

The city blurred
into soft lights and softer songs.
A tune about stars,
one about chances.
She hummed along,
He stole glances.

"So, what brought you here?"
he asked-not about the office.
"Life," she said,

"and maybe a little bit of running."

She expected judgment.
He offered silence.
The kind that lets you breathe.

She spoke of home,
not the one with walls.
He spoke of fear,
of success,
of not being enough.
Their stories spilled
like old letters
finally being read.

They laughed.
They sighed.
They didn't notice the time.
Or maybe time
had stopped noticing them.

He finally pulled over
not outside her house,
but somewhere quiet,
where goodbye
wouldn't come too fast.

"Thank you,"
she whispered,
but her eyes said more.
He nodded.
His fingers tapped the wheel,
not ready.
Not yet.

She stepped out,
the night brushing her hair
like a secret.
No words
just a look over her shoulder,
eyes holding his
a heartbeat too long.

He didn't move.
Didn't breathe.
Just watched her.
She smiled,
small and knowing,
then turned and walked away.

He sat there,
hands still on the wheel,
heart is no longer his.

"Same time tomorrow,"
he thought.
Not as a question
but as a wish,
a prayer,
a quiet promise
he hoped she'd heard
even if he never said it.

6. The Black Suit

New in love,
still walking the fragile line
between jest and confession.
She asked, half-smiling,
"So... when did you first notice me?"

He grinned,
"With a name like yours,
and a voice that echoed longer than the room allowed
you were hard to miss on the first day itself"

She raised a brow,
"Be serious."
He hesitated.
"The day you wore that suit.
Ethnic Day at work.
You were in my team
You walked that ramp like you didn't know the world
was watching."

She laughed,
"Oh god, I hated you for that.
That was not even mine,
borrowed it from my Aunt,
I don't wear suits often."

But that wasn't the only suit.
That New Year's Eve,
she asked his favorite color
not casually, but carefully,
like she was asking for a small truth
she planned to wrap herself in.

With help from her flat mates,
she got a black suit stitched,
threaded with nerves,
lined with hope,
crafted to help her feel
like she belonged in the story,
not just as a side character.

First Day of the New Year,
She waited at the restaurant,
heart pacing like a secret.
He almost walked past her
didn't recognize the version of her
who had shown up in all the ways that mattered.

"Hello?" she said.
He turned, blinked twice.
"Wait... That Was You?"

She nodded,
and he forgot how to breathe.
"You Look... Unreal!!"

In that moment,
he saw more than the suit
he saw the softness,
the effort,
the way she dressed up just for his eyes.
Not for compliments.
Not for applause.
Just for that one second of being seen.

"You Should Wear Suits More Often,"
he said, still trying to catch up
to the beauty of the moment.

She smiled
not because of the Compliment,
but because, for Once,
Being Vulnerable didn't feel like a Risk anymore.

7. The Magic in Her Touch

He was tired, the office draining his light,
Still hours to go before the night.
"You should try to sleep," she softly said,
He looked at her, weary, a shake of his head.

"In the car?" he asked, a half-hearted joke,
"I can't sleep here, I've tried, I've spoken."
She laughed, her voice like a soft melody,
"My brother swore by me, can't you see?

He'd wake me up when the stress was too much,
Said I should make a career out of my touch,
'Take this as a job,' he couldn't resist."
Even my Uncle vouch,
I give the best scalp massage, he'd insist,

He wanted to say 'no,' but there was something in her
smile,
A hope that made him stay for a while.
So he sat back, his eyes half-lidded,

And she started, her hands gentle and timid.

The moment her fingers brushed through his hair,
A calmness swept through the air.
He couldn't believe how his body sank,
Into a peaceful rhythm, no longer blank.

Five minutes, then ten and he was out,
His snoring soft, no fear, no doubt.
She kept her hand steady, not a twitch,
Waiting patiently, without a hitch.

An hour passed, he finally stirred,
His voice groggy, but his words were heard,
"How did you do it?" He asked in surprise,
"You're a magician," he said with wide eyes.

She smiled softly, her heart light and free,
"Maybe magic's real when you let it be.
It's not just the touch, but the care you give,
In quiet moments, that's when we truly live."

8. The Night His Bike Broke

The night was quiet, the world half-asleep,
Two hearts awake, in secrets deep.
Fresh in love, yet steady and true,
A story unfolding in shades of blue.

A night shift ended, the city still,
He took her riding, chasing the thrill.
No grand café, no candlelight,
Just chai and paratha under neon light.

She knew his pockets were light with change,
But never once did her love estrange.
The world may measure wealth in gold,
But she saw riches in a heart untold.

The engine sputtered, the ride stood still,
Petrol ran dry, he lost his will.
Shame burned deep, he couldn't confide,
Yet she saw through the walls he tried to hide.

She had a choice to frown, complain,
Or hold him close, ease his pain.
So with a smile, extra wide,
She walked with him, step for stride.

"I love walks," she brightly said,
Hiding the yawn, shaking her head.
A thirty-minute stretch to the station's door,
Yet she made it feel like so much more.

His hands felt empty, his pride was sore,
Yet no one had ever made him feel this *more.*
She gave, not to fix, nor to make him owe,
But so he'd never feel *less* in her glow.

The night would end, but he wasn't done,
He couldn't let go, not this one.
"A few minutes in the park?" he said,
She nodded, smiling, tilting her head.

They sat in silence, the world unseen,
A quiet corner, just hearts between.
He had so much, so much to say,
Yet no words formed, they slipped away.

And in that moment, raw and real,
His eyes betrayed what words concealed.

Tears fell freely, he couldn't hide,
Yet she just held him, arms open wide.

She wiped his tears, kissed his hand,
"I see you, I understand."
No riches, no promises, no grand display,
Just a love that whispered *"I am here to stay."*

9. 130 Rupees of Forever

They didn't walk into candlelight,
no velvet chairs,
no polished plates.
Just a pocket with **one hundred thirty rupees**
and a hunger for something more than food.

Bhelpuri for thirty,
Sweet potato for twenty,
Pani puri for forty.
A feast in paper cones,
spiced with laughter,
served under streetlights instead of chandeliers.

She knew the money was thin,
the world might call it "not enough."
But love has never been about enough,
it's about showing up
with what you have,
and who you are.

He offered her his everything,
She accepted it like treasure.
Because love is not measured in rupees,
but in the way two souls
sit side by side,
savoring simple things,
making them sacred.

And that night,
they both passed a quiet test
loyalty measured not in gold,
but in trust.
Not in price tags,
but in presence.

For real love doesn't need
a rich table to grow.
It feeds on laughter,
on promise,
on two people choosing
again and again
to show up.

10. Where Love Begins

She wasn't easy to know - not all at once,
Her laughter was loud, but her silences were fronts.
She spoke of romance like it was a game,
But deep down, she feared she'd never feel the same.

He didn't offer grand gestures or lines,
Just tea in the morning and showing up on time.
He didn't try to fix her, didn't ask why,
Just held space when she wanted to cry.

She told him once, "I'm not whole, you know
There are rooms in me where even I don't go."
He nodded, eyes quiet, didn't look away,
"I don't need all the lights. I'll sit in the gray."

He showed her patience, not pressed or loud,
The kind that speaks soft, yet feels so proud.
She found herself laughing at things that once stung,
And telling him stories she'd buried when young.

They didn't fall fast, they didn't fall blind,
They walked - step by step, leaving their bruised pasts
behind.
Two broken beginnings, stitched side by side,
Not a fairytale but something better, something wide.

A place where love wasn't perfect or neat,
But found in small things like resting your feet,
Or sleeping in cars with fingers in hair,
And waking to someone who's simply... there.

11. What We Don't Say

It happened one night, no storm, no fight,
Just a quiet distance beneath the porch light.
She laughed less that evening, eyes far away,
He noticed the silence but didn't know what to say.

He'd learned to carry without complaint,
To mask his tiredness with practiced restraint.
She'd learned to vanish in plain daylight,
Smiling through pain, keeping it light.

But love, real love, finds cracks in disguise,
It notices the trembles behind steady eyes.
He reached for her hand, her fingers withdrew,
Old reflexes returning, cold and true.

"I don't need fixing," she suddenly said,
Her voice was low, like she feared where it led.
"I know," he replied, with no defense,
"I just wanted to sit in your silence, not make sense."

She looked at him then, truly looked,
Saw the boy who bore burdens no one else took.
The man who never learned to ask for more,
Because asking once meant watching doors close before.

They didn't solve it, didn't pretend to try,
They sat beneath stars in a mutual sigh.
Two people with ghosts, not running away
Just choosing, instead, to softly stay.

It wasn't loud love, or some grand parade,
But the kind that stays when you're unafraid.
To let someone see the mess and the ache,
And know this time it won't make them break.

12. A Table for Two

The days felt long,
the nights unsure,
Apart for Diwali,
but love stayed pure.
She flew back home,
the festive light,
Yet left his world a shade less bright.

Now she's here,
across the flame,
A beating heart that calls her name.
He wears the shirt she once bestowed,
Freshly groomed and perfumed just as she loved.

Their laughter hums,
their voices play,
Like autumn leaves that dance, then stay.
A table set,
her favorite place,
Two souls wrapped in love's embrace.

No grand confessions,
none were due,
Just stolen glances - soft and true.
A love so new,
yet deep and wide,
Once coworkers, now side by side.

Tonight's not about the food or wine,
But finding home in each new sign.
A touch, a smile, a knowing glance,
A love so young, yet made to last.

13. The Night the Boy Disappeared

He spoke one evening, voice barely there,
Like opening a wound without knowing where.
They were driving, the world dim and still,
The kind of quiet that bends time to will.

"I was Sixteen when I stopped being a kid,"
He said, not looking at her as he did.
"My dad sat me down, eyes full of rain,
Told me the business was gone, just gone, plain."

No warning, no safety net, just a fall,
And suddenly, he was the man of it all.
Woke up at five, worked until late,
Homework at midnight, sleep had to wait.

He didn't cry, not that day, not once.
Just swallowed his fear and did what he must.
Sold the house to pay for the bills,
Lied to his friends about weekend thrills.

Birthdays became gas money,
New shoes? A joke, too funny.
And when his mom cried behind the door,
He stayed outside, pretending to snore.

"I never blamed them," he said, soft and sure,
"But I never healed either... I just learned to endure."
She reached for his hand, held it tight,
No pity, just presence, like moonlight.

For once, he didn't need to be strong,
Didn't have to prove he belonged.
She didn't speak, didn't fill the air
She just *stayed*, and that was rare.

And in that silence, something began,
Not the fixing of a broken man
But the moment he was seen, truly clear.
The boy he buried... was finally near.

14. The Sound of the Car

She told him one night, curled up small,
The moonlight slicing shadows on the wall.
Her voice was calm, but her hands betrayed,
Fingers fidgeting like a child afraid.

"I used to wait by the door at Five,"
She began, "just to see if he'd arrive.
My dad... he was never on time,
But I thought if I waited, he'd read that as a sign."

She'd sit with a book she pretended to read,
Staring at roads that never paid heed.
Every car that passed made her heart rise,
Every silence, another hope dies.

"One day," she whispered, "I stopped waiting."
Her voice cracked on words she'd been hating.
"I was eleven. And that was the first time
I chose silence instead of trying to climb."

He listened, still, breath held like thread,
Not interrupting, just turning his head.
"I still remember the sound of his Car," she said,
"When he left for good. No goodbye. Just dread."

Her mother had cried in the kitchen that night,
But no one explained, no one made it right.
She learned that love meant *leaving first,*
That softness was weakness, and trust was a curse.

"I built walls after that. Pretty ones too.
Smiled a lot. Made sure no one knew.
But sometimes," she said, voice thick and slow,
"I still flinch when someone walks out the door."

He reached for her then not like a savior,
But as someone who knew that kind of flavor.
Not to fix. Not to soothe with a lie.
Just to hold her, and let her cry.

And in that night, they stitched another seam
Two broken pasts sharing one quiet dream.
Not of perfect homes or fairy-tale ends,
But of becoming each other's safest friends.

15. Her Fierce Choice

It was an inter-caste love.
But that was never the hurdle.

The world pointed instead
to what he didn't have
no house of his own,
no fancy car to drive,
no glitter of security
that families cling to like prayer beads.

She knew this
from the start.
Because he never hid.
He never lied.
And isn't that what love deserves?
truth,
naked and unpolished.

When the time came,
questions rose sharp,

judgments pressed heavy,
but she stood
unmoved,
unbothered.

Because how could she let him
be weighed on scales
that never measures the soul?
How could she let them
reduce a man
to what he owns,
when she had already seen
the wealth he carried
in his heart?

She saw it
the heart of gold,
fierce in its will to provide,
gentle in its loyalty,
unyielding in its love.

He was not a checklist.
He was not a possession.
He was her companion,
her best friend,
her once-in-a-lifetime.

And so she chose
loudly,
bravely,
fully
to stand beside him.

Because sometimes
the deepest rebellion of love
is refusing the world's measures,
and declaring instead:
A man is enough,
not for what he owns,
but for how he loves.

16. The Man with a Heart of Gold

I married a man with empty hands,
No silver, no land, no grand demands.
But his heart gleamed with golden light,
A love so deep, so pure, so right.

He saw the scars I tried to hide,
The little girl still lost inside.
With patient hands, with tender grace,
He kissed the wounds time can't erase.

He made me feel both strong and small,
A woman fierce, a child enthralled.
Wrapped in his arms, I feel so free,
Yet safe, as if he carries me.

He soothes my fears, he dries my tears,
He quiets all my restless years.
No tantrum shakes his steady ground,
He holds me close, he sticks around.

He calls me Begum, he pampers me,
Yet lets me fly, yet lets me be.
Through every doubt, through every storm,
His love is home - his love is warm.

He's seen my worst, yet never strays,
He loves me still, in all my ways.
He lifts me up, he sets me free,
He makes me love the *whole* of me.

And oh, of all the gifts so fine,
His Chai is magic - sweet, divine.
A cup so rich, so brewed with care,
Just like his love, beyond compare.
I married a man with a heart of Gold.

17. Not the Same Rain

It was supposed to be a half-day.
Just work.
Just chores.
Just ordinary.

But then
the skies broke open.
Rain.
Pouring like cats and dogs.

We were on a bike.
No car anymore
That chapter closed.
Just two of us,
two wheels,
and a storm.

We stopped.
Ten minutes under some shade.
Thinking

it'll pass.
But when we rode again...
the rain?
It was merciless.

Calls from the office kept buzzing,
but how do you show up
soaked to the bone?
So we gave in.
Took the leave.

Not the cozy kind.
Not the fake sick day kind.
But the kind of leave
life hands you
with a hidden lesson tucked inside.

And that day
I realized.
Rain is not joy for everyone.

As a kid,
I loved it.
I ran in it,
laughed in it,
called it magic.

But adulthood gave me new lenses.
Through them I saw
two-wheelers stopping,
people drenched,
looking for shelter.
Saw an old man on a cycle,
trying to cover himself,
failing against the storm.
Saw fruit sellers,
vegetable vendors,
scrambling to save their livelihood
from washing away.

And that's when it hit me
The rain is never one story.

For some
It's poetry.
For some
its survival.
One sky.
One storm.
A thousand different realities
falling at once.

18. When Rain Turns to Roads

That day in the rain,
my eyes flowed like a river.
Not from joy
but from a truth I had never tasted it.
The feeling was new,
uncomfortable,
sharp as lightning.

And in that moment,
soaked to the bone,
we decided:
We need a car.

Because when two souls decide
with pure, clear intention
the Universe listens.
It rewards sooner than expected.

Five months.

That's all it took.
Five months of ruthless saving.
No shopping.
No outside food.
No extras.
Every coin guarded,
every note folded tight with purpose.

Two kids,
mid twenties,
barely one year married.
But we made it.
We bought our first car.

From the test drive
to the delivery,
It felt unreal.
Not grand.
Not show-stopping.
But ours.
Completely ours.

And sometimes
life teaches you lessons
just so you remember your worth.
Just so you believe
in the magic of timing,

in the beauty of patience,
in the miracles that come
when love and determination
hold hands.

19. 130 Rupees to The JW Marriott

Four and a half years...
That company was my beginning.
My grind.
My fire.
It gave me bitter-sweet memories,
and lessons carved into my bones.

And when the farewell came
Grand,
Glowing,
Loud,
Overflowing
I cried
not softly,
but with every corner of my being.

Then home.
And waiting there
Another surprise.

My favorite cake.
A bouquet.
And a hug that didn't let go
until my heart slowed down.

He didn't ask.
He didn't need to.
He just knew.
And the river of tears came again
this time not from loss,
but gratitude.
Happy tears.
Grateful tears.

I told him everything
the farewell,
the decorations,
the laughter,
the warmth,
the gifts.
My eyes lit up.
And his
his eyes softened.

A man like him,
kind to his core,
wanted to honor them too.

To celebrate the ones
who celebrated me.

Without a pause,
without a thought,
He chose the best place in the city.
The JW Marriott.

And me?
The woman in me couldn't help
but remember
the boy I first met.
The one who once took me out on a date
with 130 rupees in his pocket.
Bhelpuri.
Sweet potato.
Pani puri.
And a heart richer
than any man in the room.

Life whispered its quiet truth that night:
Time changes.
Money flows.
But Love
Real Love
never needed currency to survive.

For I learned
a man is never measured
by what fills his pockets,
but by what he offers when they are empty.

20. Already Enough

Two days before my birthday
I quit.
Closed the chapter on a decade-long corporate life.
Not with fear,
but with fire.
To chase what my heart
and soul
were always whispering.

A quick plan.
A trip.
Manali.
Our safe space,
our memory keeper,
a place that greets us
like an old friend
every single time.

We left early morning
birthday sunrise on the road.

The trip? Magical.
The cottage? Ours.
An entire home wrapped in quiet,
and Cooper, our furry boy
already approving,
tail wagging in lush gardens,
claiming the space as his own.

Life has come full circle.
From dating on coins and courage,
to this
breathing in comfort
We built it together.

We stopped by our favorite bakery,
picked some cupcakes.
Because this birthday
was different.
Not about noise,
but about meaning.
And good food
It always makes life softer.

At 11:11,
on my birthday,
I had no wishes left.
Not because I lacked dreams,

but because I was full.
Completely full.

That's when I knew
I had made it.
Not rich in money.
Rich in love.
Rich in freedom.
Rich in moments like this.

21. What is Love?

Love is not about fancy dates.
Love for me
is eating maggi at 3 a.m.,
after bingeing a Netflix series together,
sleepy-eyed, yet smiling.

Love is not about coffee dates.
Love for me
is when he learned to sip tea
not because he needed it,
but because I did.

Love is not about luxury vacations.
Love for me
is the quietest joy
an ice-cream drive
after weekend dinner,
wind in our hair,
hearts at peace.

Love is not about buying a big house.
Love for me
is building a home together
brick by brick of trust,
rooms without judgment,
a space where we can be
our raw, unfiltered selves.

Love is not about expensive gifts.
Love for me
is his voice steady and certain:
"Follow your passion.
Be free.
Be you."

Love is not about who said sorry first.
Love for me
is knowing that even in anger,
He cares.
That love doesn't disappear
in the heat of a fight.

Love is not about marrying a well-settled man.
Love for me
is standing in his struggle,
hand in hand,
building dreams out of nothing.

Love is not about happily ever after.
Love for me
is showing up,
every single day,
choosing to grow,
choosing to heal,
choosing each other
again, and again.

www.ingramcontent.com/pod-product-compliance
Lightning Source LLC
Chambersburg PA
CBHW060353050426
42449CB00011B/2967